GUESS THE
POKÉMON

Written by Glenn Dakin

INTRODUCTION

Test your Pokémon knowledge!

From the deepest sea to the darkest cave, or even just hanging out in your backyard—Pokémon can be found everywhere!

This book will introduce you to wonderful Pokémon from all of the currently known regions of the Pokémon world. Learn fun facts about Pokémon, big and small, and see if you have what it takes to guess all the different types of Pokémon.

Ready? Let's Go!

How to Play "Guess The Pokémon"

Prove you are a great Trainer by looking carefully at the Pokémon shape, reading the clue, and turning the page to reveal the Pokémon! Can you and your friends guess all the Pokémon?

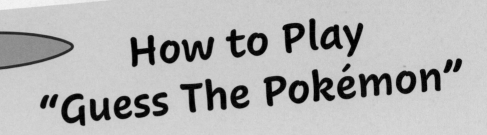

GUESS THE POKÉMON

• TURN THE PAGE TO FIND OUT! •

IT'S... Pikachu!

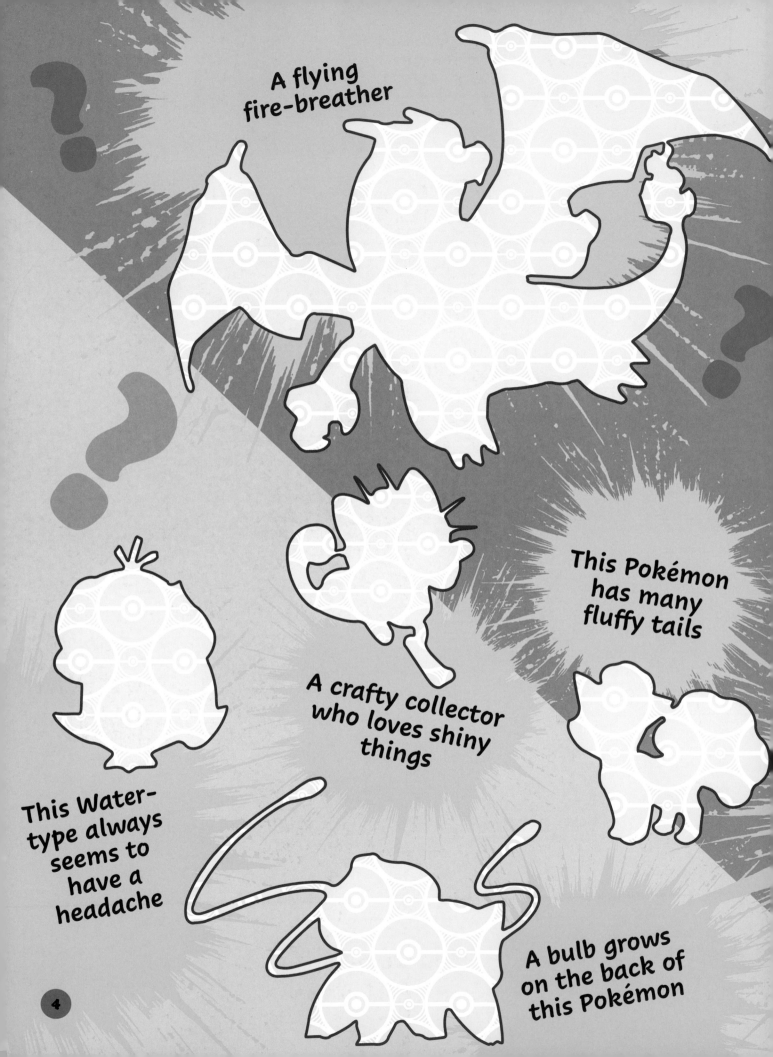

A flying
fire-breather

This Pokémon
has many
fluffy tails

A crafty collector
who loves shiny
things

This Water-
type always
seems to
have a
headache

A bulb grows
on the back of
this Pokémon

4

This Pokémon can make shadows move

Sploosh! This Pokémon makes a huge splash

GUESS THE POKÉMON

TURN THE PAGE TO FIND OUT!

A Mouse Pokémon with Electric-type moves

This Water-type glides across the sea

Giant petals sprout from this Pokémon

IT'S . . .

CHARIZARD

Type: Fire-Flying

Charizard can melt boulders with its red-hot breath. Sometimes forest fires are caused by this Flame Pokémon.

MEOWTH

Type: Normal

When Meowth is feeling happy, it might reveal its shiny treasure collection to a Trainer.

PSYDUCK

Type: Water

This Duck Pokémon gets annoying headaches. Psyduck can get some relief from the pain by releasing its strange psychic power.

BULBASAUR

Type: Grass-Poison

This Pokémon is born with a bulb growing on its back that, over time, gradually grows larger.

VULPIX

Type: Fire

While young, this Fox Pokémon has six beautiful tails. As it gets older, more and more fluffy tails grow.

SQUIRTLE

Type: Water

Squirtle is a Tiny Turtle Pokémon. It can retract its neck into its shell and send out a powerful jet of water to drench anyone in its path.

GENGAR

Type: Ghost-Poison

Gengar loves to cause mischief. It creates laughing shadows that move around in the light of the full moon.

LAPRAS

Type: Water-Ice

This intelligent and kindhearted Pokémon sings a beautiful song as it floats through the waves.

PIKACHU

Type: Electric

Pikachu can send out sizzling electric bolts. It stores electricity in its soft, stretchy cheek sacs.

VILEPLUME

Type: Grass-Poison

Vileplume's petals are pretty but dangerous! They are filled with poisonous pollen that can be shaken out in thick clouds.

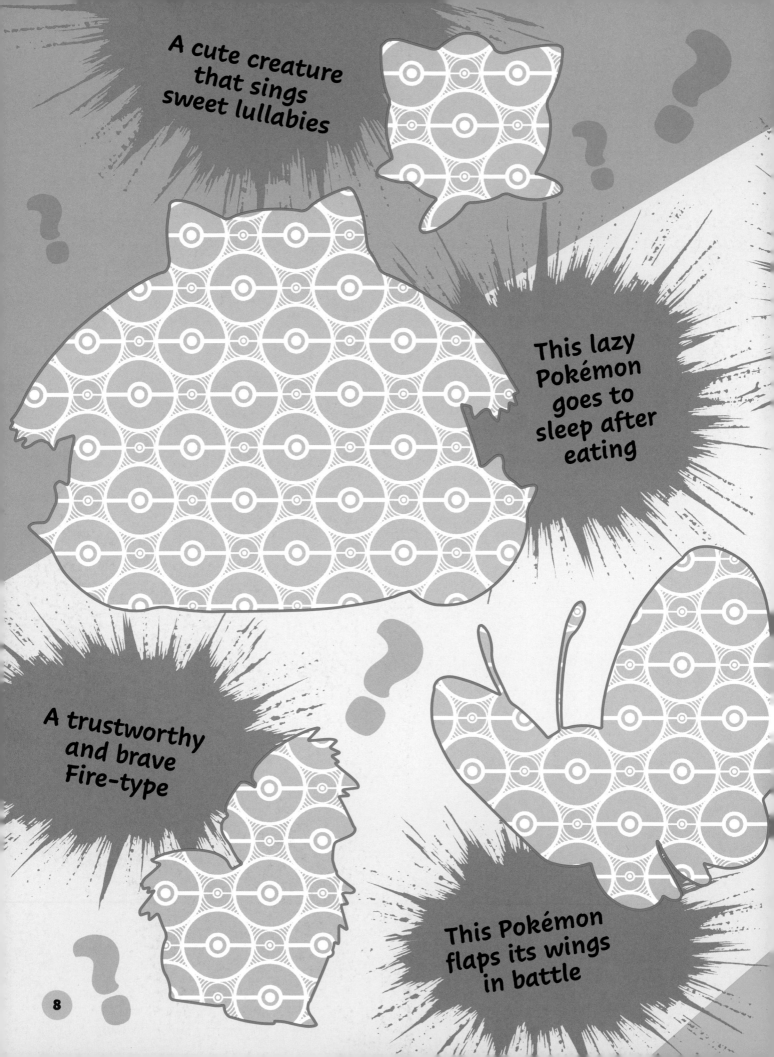

A deep-digging team of three

The weakest Pokémon of all

GUESS THE POKÉMON

TURN THE PAGE TO FIND OUT!

This rotten Pokémon is full of poisonous gas

A rarely found Fairy-type Pokémon

This Pokémon does not evolve

A fluffy Evolution Pokémon

IT'S . . .

JIGGLYPUFF

Type: Normal-Fairy

Jigglypuff uses its amazing lung capacity to keep singing lullabies until all of its enemies have fallen asleep.

SNORLAX

Type: Normal

Known as the Sleeping Pokémon, Snorlax likes to eat at least 880 pounds of food a day.

GROWLITHE

Type: Fire

This courageous Pokémon is a fiery fighter. It will stand up to any foe, no matter how big or small.

BUTTERFREE

Type: Bug-Flying

This Pokémon is great in battle. Butterfree can release toxic dust in the air by flapping its wings extra fast.

DUGTRIO

Type: Ground

A solo Diglett joins two pals to become a Dugtrio. This Mole Pokémon can dig up to 60 miles underground and cause huge earthquakes.

MAGIKARP

Type: Water

Regarded as one of the weakest and most pathetic Pokémon, this floppy creature evolves into the fierce Gyarados.

CLEFAIRY

Type: Fairy

Adorable Clefairy gather to dance under the full moon. It is said happiness will come to those who are lucky enough to see them.

KOFFING

Type: Poison

Koffing loves the reek of rotting trash! It is drawn to garbage dumps and polluted air.

MEW

Type: Psychic

Mew's short, beautiful hair is so fine it can only be seen under a microscope.

EEVEE

Type: Normal

Due to Eevee's unusual genetic makeup, it can alter its body to adapt to the world around it.

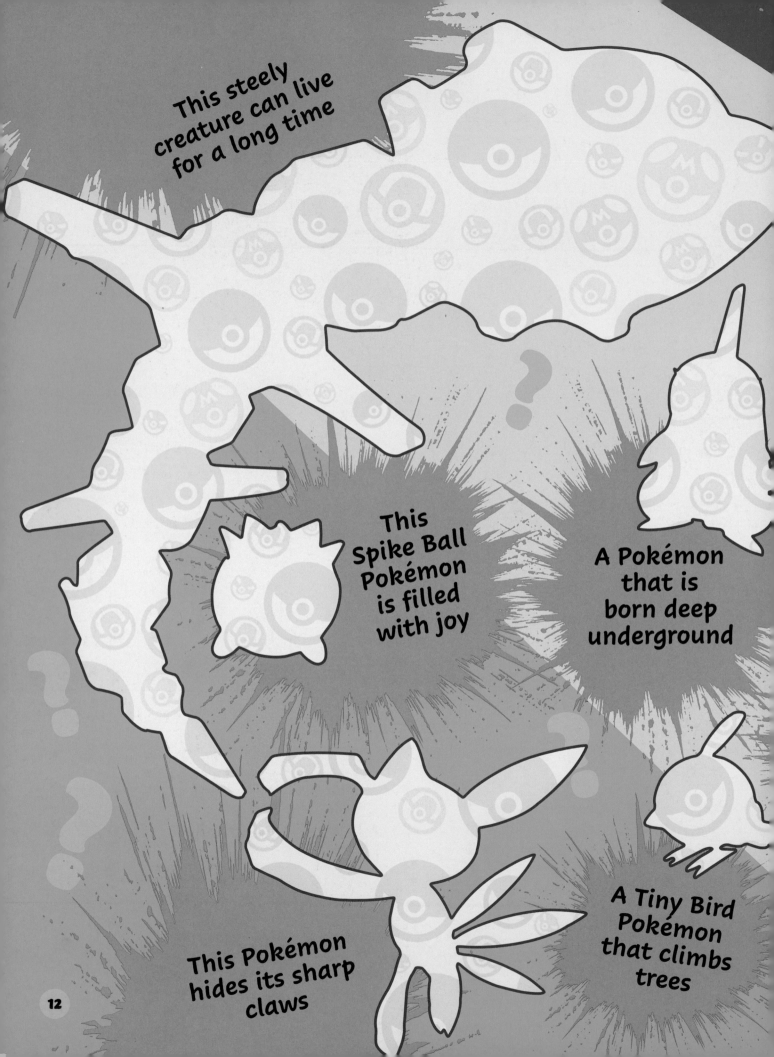

This steely creature can live for a long time

This Spike Ball Pokémon is filled with joy

A Pokémon that is born deep underground

This Pokémon hides its sharp claws

A Tiny Bird Pokémon that climbs trees

This Psychic-type hates being surprised

A Pokémon disguised as a tree

An easygoing swimmer that bumps into boats

This Pokémon carries food all day

Watch out for this Pokémon's squirts of ink

GUESS THE POKÉMON · TURN THE PAGE TO FIND OUT!

IT'S . . .

STEELIX
Type: Steel-Ground
If Steelix lives for more than 100 years, its body transforms to become tougher and diamond-like.

TOGEPI
Type: Fairy
Togepi's shell is filled with happiness. It is ready to share its joy when discovered. Trainers can gain good luck by treating it kindly.

LARVITAR
Type: Rock-Ground
After Larvitar has eaten a large mountain of soil, it falls asleep for a long time. While it sleeps, it grows.

SNEASEL
Type: Dark-Ice
Not to be messed with, this Pokémon can shock a foe with just the sudden reveal of its sharp claws.

NATU
Type: Psychic-Flying
Natu likes to look for tasty sprouts to peck. Its wings are so small it can't fly, so it has learned to be a great climber instead.

WOBBUFFET

Type: Psychic

A favorite of Team Rocket, Wobbuffet can inflate its body to look bigger and tougher when threatened.

SUDOWOODO

Type: Rock

This Imitation Pokémon copies a tree to avoid being noticed. It dislikes water and will run away from the rain.

DELIBIRD

Type: Ice-Flying

This life-saving Pokémon delivers food whenever and wherever it is needed. It has fed many lost, starving people and Pokémon.

QUAGSIRE

Type: Water-Ground

A carefree Water Fish Pokémon, Quagsire often bumps into obstacles in the water but doesn't seem to mind.

OCTILLERY

Type: Water

Octillery chooses to hide in rocky crags or pots for protection. It squirts ink from the shadows before making its attack.

A sweet-smelling Pokémon with sharp thorns

At times called the most beautiful Pokémon of all

This Pokémon can feel emotions in others

Happy music brings this Pokémon energy

This Pokémon can see well in the dark

A super-speedy Electric-type

GUESS THE POKÉMON

TURN THE PAGE TO FIND OUT!

Brr! This Ice-type is a sure sign of snow

This Pokémon can survive in dirty water

Whipping up a sandstorm is easy for this Pokémon

A Pokémon with a hollow body

IT'S...

ROSELIA

Type: Grass-Poison

The healthier Roselia is, the stronger its amazing scent. But this Thorn Pokémon has a dangerous side with some prickly attack moves.

MILOTIC

Type: Water

This Tender Pokémon has inspired many artists with its delicate beauty. It can calm others' hostile emotions.

RALTS

Type: Psychic-Fairy

This sensitive Pokémon hides away at the first sign of a fight. Its body heats up if its horns sense warm feelings in others.

LUDICOLO

Type: Water-Grass

Cheerful and fun-loving, Ludicolo finds its cells charged up by the rhythm of festive dancing.

NOCTOWL

Type: Normal-Flying

A sharp-eyed Noctowl can see in the murkiest light! This Pokémon can also twist its head to see behind its back.

MANECTRIC

Type: Electric

Manectric can use its electric energy to move quickly. It also uses electricity to heal wounds faster.

SNORUNT

Type: Ice

The Snow Hat Pokémon eats snow and ice. If one is seen happily bouncing at midnight, snow is sure to fall!

CORPHISH

Type: Water

Called the Ruffian Pokémon, Corphish has a strong survival instinct. It's tough and can thrive in the foulest waters.

FLYGON

Type: Ground-Dragon

This Mystic Pokémon does not like to be seen by others. It can even create a sandstorm to stay out of sight.

DUSCLOPS

Type: Ghost

Dusclops sucks things inside its empty body as though it were a black hole. What happens inside is still a mystery!

A high-flier that rides the sea breeze

A unique Pokémon who can control machines

This Pokémon can spin on its foot to move

GUESS THE POKÉMON

TURN THE PAGE TO FIND OUT!

A mysterious Pokémon that appears in ancient ruins

This Frost Tree Pokémon absorbs water from snow

This slippery Sea Slug changes shape to suit its habitat

IT'S . . .

LUCARIO

Type: Fighting-Steel
Lucario can control auras and fire them at an opponent in a powerful wave. This Pokémon trusts only Trainers with justice in their hearts.

GARCHOMP

Type: Dragon-Ground
Garchomp is the Mach Pokémon, which means it can fly at the speed of sound. Now that's fast! When it's not flying, Garchomp makes its home inside a volcano.

SEEDOT

Type: Grass
An Acorn Pokémon, Seedot pretends to be a nut. This prankster moves suddenly to surprise other Pokémon that are out foraging for food.

LEAFEON

Type: Grass
Leafeon is one of the many evolved forms of Eevee. Its unique scent is used to make a popular brand of perfume.

ROTOM

Type: Electric-Ghost

Rotom is attracted to electricity. Its plasma body can take over many different machines to surprise the users!

WINGULL

Type: Water-Flying

Wingull soars above the waves, gliding on the sea breeze. It builds its nest on high, steep cliffs overlooking the ocean.

BALTOY

Type: Ground-Psychic

The Clay Doll Pokémon constantly spins to move. It can whirl on its foot or upside down on its pointy head.

BRONZOR

Type: Steel-Psychic

The pattern on Bronzor's body is a source of great mystery. Stories say that polishing Bronzor makes its surface reflect the truth.

SNOVER

Type: Grass-Ice

This Pokémon lives in the chilly climate of snowy mountains. It can grow tasty berries that are like ice pops around its belly.

SHELLOS (WEST SEA)

Type: Water

This Pokémon can vary in shape and color depending on the warmth of the water it lives in. A Shellos from the cold East Sea is blue and a Shellos that lives in the warm West Sea is pink.

23

IT'S . . . !

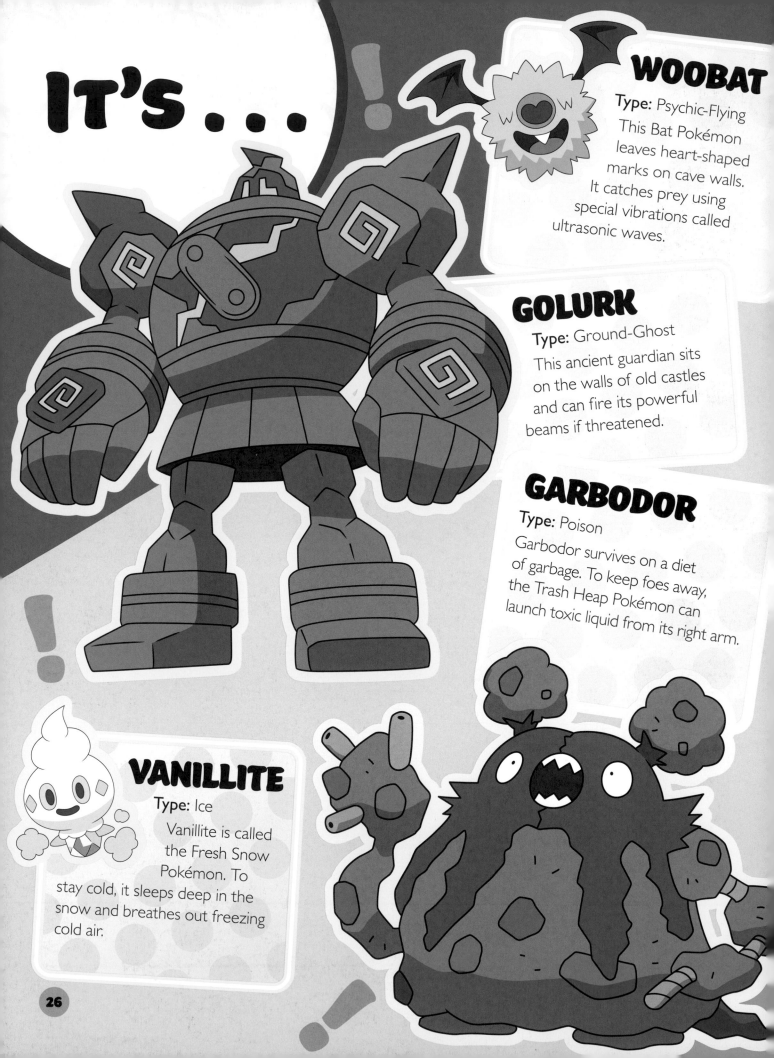

WOOBAT

Type: Psychic-Flying

This Bat Pokémon leaves heart-shaped marks on cave walls. It catches prey using special vibrations called ultrasonic waves.

GOLURK

Type: Ground-Ghost

This ancient guardian sits on the walls of old castles and can fire its powerful beams if threatened.

GARBODOR

Type: Poison

Garbodor survives on a diet of garbage. To keep foes away, the Trash Heap Pokémon can launch toxic liquid from its right arm.

VANILLITE

Type: Ice

Vanillite is called the Fresh Snow Pokémon. To stay cold, it sleeps deep in the snow and breathes out freezing cold air.

LIEPARD

Type: Dark

Looks aren't everything. Liepard has gorgeous fur, but its moody personality can be quite ugly.

KLINK

Type: Steel

These two minigears interlock best with each other. They are like twins and go everywhere together.

MINCCINO

Type: Normal

Minccino boasts about its fluffy tail to other Pokémon. It uses the brush-like tail to keep everything squeaky-clean.

DEINO

Type: Dark-Dragon

This Pokémon uses its mouth to learn about the world around it. Deino can't see, so it nibbles everything to find out what it is.

RUFFLET

Type: Normal-Flying

Rufflet faces foes without fear, but it is a sore loser! If Rufflet loses a battle, it throws a big tantrum.

MAMOSWINE

Type: Ice-Ground

This Twin Tusk Pokémon has special tusks that grow longer and thicker as the weather gets colder.

Eyelike patterns are hidden inside this Pokémon's ears

A Playful leaf-chewer that likes a fight

This Pokémon can fire electrified fur

This Pokémon attacks its enemies in the dark

A trio of buzzing nectar carriers

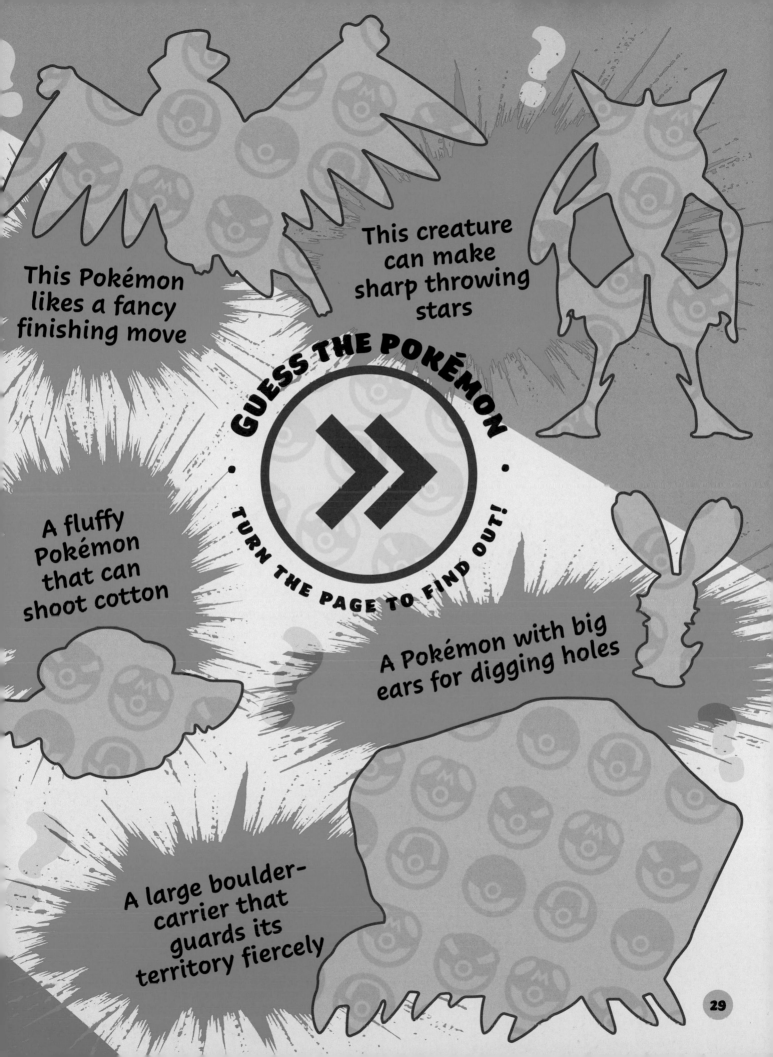

This Pokémon likes a fancy finishing move

This creature can make sharp throwing stars

GUESS THE POKÉMON

TURN THE PAGE TO FIND OUT!

A fluffy Pokémon that can shoot cotton

A Pokémon with big ears for digging holes

A large boulder-carrier that guards its territory fiercely

It's . . .

MEOWSTIC

Type: Psychic

If threatened, Meowstic raises its ears. The eyeball patterns inside its ears contain psychic power strong enough to tear a tanker apart.

GALVANTULA

Type: Bug-Electric

Galvantula can leave an opponent powerless and unable to move for three days by launching its special electrified fur at them.

PANCHAM

Type: Fighting

A Playful Pokémon, Pancham can't help but smile. It glares at other Pokémon when it wants to be taken seriously.

NOIVERN

Type: Flying-Dragon

This Sound Wave Pokémon is fierce! It surprises its foes in the dark, attacking them with ultrasonic waves.

COMBEE

Type: Bug-Flying

This Pokémon comes as a set of three, and they work together to gather nectar. They are a great team, but feeding time can be a bit tricky because each one prefers a different kind of nectar.

HAWLUCHA

Type: Fighting-Flying

This Wrestling Pokémon wears its opponent out with its acrobatic moves. It strikes a flashy pose before finishing a battle.

GRENINJA

Type: Water-Dark

This Pokémon appears and disappears like a silent ninja. Its water throwing stars can split metal in two!

COTTONEE

Type: Grass-Fairy

This Cotton Puff Pokémon is as light as a cloud. If it gets caught in a hurricane, Cottonee could be blown to the other side of the world!

BUNNELBY

Type: Normal

Bunnelby can dig a burrow 33 feet deep in just one night using its special ears.

CRUSTLE

Type: Bug-Rock

Crustle prefers dry weather. On rainy days, it will hide in its boulder and refuse to come out.

This Pokémon lives in groups of around 20

A pollen-loving Pokémon with a sweet tooth

A tough Battery Pokémon

This Pokémon rattles its scaly tail to scare opponents

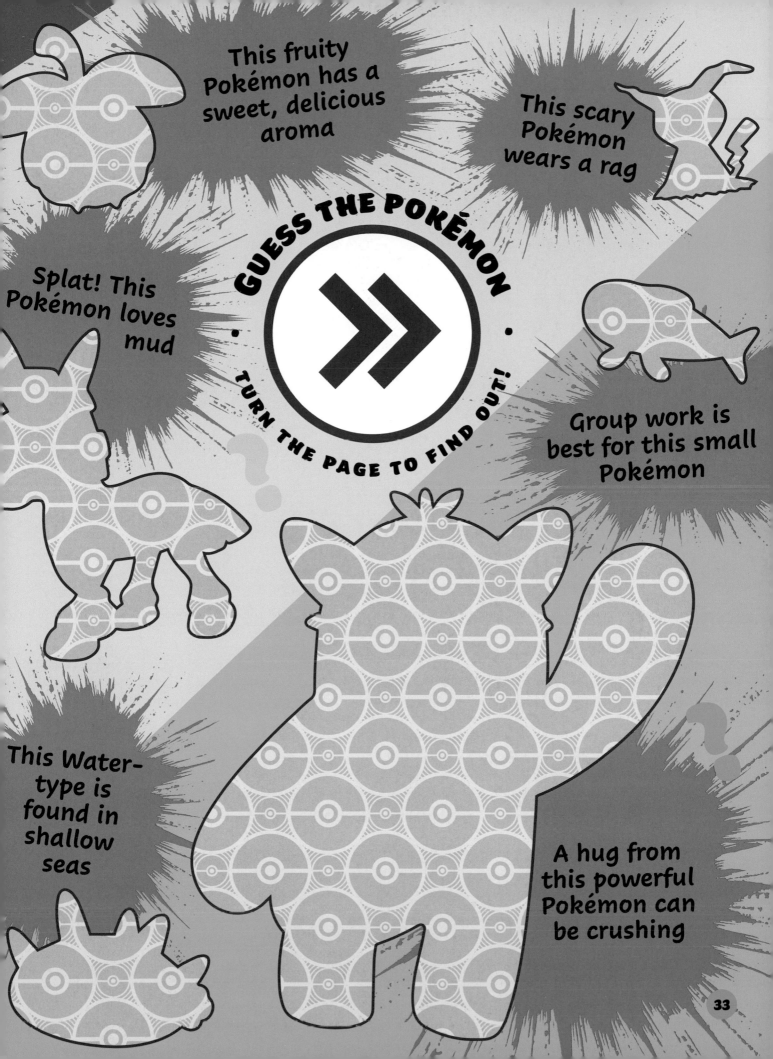

This fruity Pokémon has a sweet, delicious aroma

This scary Pokémon wears a rag

GUESS THE POKÉMON
TURN THE PAGE TO FIND OUT!

Splat! This Pokémon loves mud

Group work is best for this small Pokémon

This Water-type is found in shallow seas

A hug from this powerful Pokémon can be crushing

IT'S . . .

CUTIEFLY

Type: Bug-Fairy

This Bee Fly Pokémon can read an opponent's aura to predict what their next battle move will be.

PASSIMIAN

Type: Fighting

This loyal squad member is happy being part of a team. It follows the boss's orders to search for berries.

CHARJABUG

Type: Bug-Electric

Charjabug is a Battery Pokémon with a tough shell. To attack it can shoot electricity from its jaws.

KOMMO-O

Type: Dragon-Fighting

This Scaly Pokémon puts on a noisy display of rattling scales to scare its foes. Only those who stand firm will be allowed to duel with it.

BOUNSWEET

Type: Grass

Everything about this cute fruit makes it a tasty snack to Bird Pokémon. Even its sweat smells delicious!

MIMIKYU

Type: Ghost-Fairy

Mimikyu tries to look like Pikachu to appear less scary, but the costume just makes it look creepier!

MUDBRAY

Type: Ground

A Donkey Pokémon, Mudbray is super-strong. It can carry up to 50 times its own weight.

WISHIWASHI

Type: Water

Wishiwashi is weak on its own. But when it teams up with other Wishiwashi Pokémon, the group can tackle deadly opponents.

PYUKUMUKU

Type: Water

This Sea Cucumber Pokémon keeps its skin moist with slime. That way it can stay on land without drying out.

BEWEAR

Type: Normal-Fighting

This Strong Arm Pokémon can be dangerous! Bewear likes to give its friends a big hug, but sometimes it can't control its own strength.

This fiery opponent has large, sharp fangs

A Pokémon that can be spun into glossy yarn

GUESS THE POKÉMON

»

TURN THE PAGE TO FIND OUT!

This Fighting-type uses a leek as a sword

This creature lives inside an apple

A restless Pokémon that enjoys running around

It's . . .

GROOKEY

Type: Grass

The beat of Grookey's stick creates sound waves that spread fresh energy to all growing plants and flowers around it.

WOOLOO

Type: Normal

This Sheep Pokémon has wonderfully soft wool. Its coat protects it from falls from great heights, allowing it to get back on its feet unharmed.

PIDOVE

Type: Normal-Flying

This sincere Tiny Pigeon Pokémon always follows people around, hoping to get crumbs of food.

ZACIAN

Type: Fairy-Steel

A legendary hero, this Warrior Pokémon absorbs metal particles. It turns the particles into weapons for battle.

DOTTLER

Type: Bug-Psychic

Dottler has a secret life. It hides in its shell, hardly ever moving. While in its shell, it uses psychic powers to monitor the outside world.

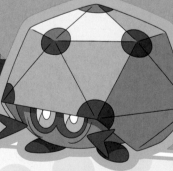

CENTISKORCH

Type: Fire-Bug

This Radiator Pokémon uses its fiery form like a burning whip and gives its foes a lashing they will never forget.

ELDEGOSS

Type: Grass

A big ball of fluffy seeds is attached to this kind Pokémon. It plants natural goodness wherever it goes.

SIRFETCH'D

Type: Fighting

Sir fetch'd is the hero of many battles, but it cannot be victorious forever. It retires from dueling and glory when the leek it brandishes withers.

GALARIAN ZIGZAGOON

Type: Dark-Normal

The Zigzagoon is a Tiny Raccoon Pokémon. Native to Galar, the Galarian Zigzagoon has a fiesty personality!

APPLIN

Type: Grass-Dragon

An apple is a clever hiding place for this Apple Core Pokémon. It stops its natural enemies, Bird Pokémon, from finding it.

A Pokémon with a copper body

This Pokémon is a talented tap dancer

Boo hoo! This woeful weeper makes others cry too

A Puppy Pokémon that herds others

Chomp! This Pokémon has a strong bite

This Pokémon is sweet and creamy

This Pokémon goes on destructive rampages

This Cheeky Pokémon eats berries

GUESS THE POKÉMON

TURN THE PAGE TO FIND OUT!

Eek! This Ghost-type is full of supernatural energy

A nibbler that makes its own electricity

41

It's . . .

MR. RIME
Type: Ice-Psychic
Mr. Rime likes to put on a fancy show. It waves its ice cane in time to its dazzling tap dancing.

CUFANT
Type: Steel
This strong Pokémon can easily carry five tons of weight without a care in the world. That's the same as carrying more than 755 Pikachu!

SOBBLE
Type: Water
Sobble's tears unleash the chemical power of 100 onions. This makes the eyes of anyone nearby well up.

YAMPER
Type: Electric
This Pokémon runs around to create electricity in its tail. After work, Yamper enjoys a tasty treat.

ALCREMIE
Type: Fairy
This Pokémon will treat a trusted Trainer to a generous helping of sweet berries and cream.

DREDNAW
Type: Water-Rock
This hard-shelled tough Pokémon can rapidly extend its neck to snap distant prey. Its strong fangs can even bite through steel rods!

GYARADOS

Type: Water-Flying

Super aggressive, this Atrocious Pokémon can burn any target to a frazzle with its searing Hyper Beam.

SKWOVET

Type: Normal

Skwovet lives in the Galar Region. It gets nervous if it doesn't have at least one berry in its cheeks.

CURSOLA

Type: Ghost

The core of this Coral Pokémon is protected by ghostly ectoplasm. If anyone touches Cursola, they become stiff as a stone!

MORPEKO

Type: Electric-Dark

Morpeko stores seeds in pocket-like pouches on its belly. It gobbles up the seeds to generate electricity.

A Big Rock that can kick

This Fighting-type can punch, chop, and thump

A haunted Pokémon living in a teacup

GUESS THE POKÉMON

TURN THE PAGE TO FIND OUT!

This crafty Dark-type steals from others

This Pokémon has a mountain of coal

IT'S...

EISCUE

Type: Ice

This Pokémon drifted in on the ocean from a frozen place. It keeps its head under ice at all times to stay chilled out.

ZAMAZENTA

Type: Fighting-Steel

Equipped with its impressive shield, Zamazenta is ready for battle. In ancient times, it fought alongside a king to defend Galar.

SCORBUNNY

Type: Fire

This Rabbit Pokémon warms up by running around. The unique pads on its nose and feet get especially hot.

CORVIKNIGHT

Type: Flying-Steel

Corviknight is a master of the skies. The night-dark sheen of its steel feathers strikes awe into its foes.

ARROKUDA

Type: Water

If it notices any kind of movement, Arrokuda swims straight for it. It snaps up prey with its powerful jaws.

MACHAMP

Type: Fighting

Machamp reacts fist first. This four-armed fighter never lets up with its battering blows!

STONJOURNER

Type: Rock

Stonjourner watches the sun go down from a grassy plain. Once a year, it meets other Stonjourner to form a mysterious circle.

SINISTEA

Type: Ghost

A ghostly tale says that this Black Tea Pokémon was created when a lonely spirit possessed a cold, leftover cup of tea!

NICKIT

Type: Dark

This cunning Fox Pokémon is a master of stealing food. It uses the soft pads of its feet to silently sneak up to food stores.

COALOSSAL

Type: Rock-Fire

This Pokémon prefers a peaceful life but doesn't like it when people vandalize mines. It fights back by breathing scorching-hot flames.

DK | Penguin Random House

Editor Nicole Reynolds
Designers James McKeag and Thelma-Jane Robb
Senior Production Editor Marc Staples
Senior Production Controller Lloyd Robertson
Managing Editor Paula Regan
Managing Art Editor Jo Connor
Publishing Director Mark Searle

DK would like to thank Hank Woon and the rest of the team at The Pokémon Company International. Also, at DK, Julia March and Tori Kosara for editorial assistance and Jennette ElNaggar and Ruth Amos for proofreading.

First American Edition, 2021
Published in the United States by DK Publishing
1450 Broadway, Suite 801, New York, NY 10018

Page design copyright © 2021 Dorling Kindersley Limited
DK, a Division of Penguin Random House LLC
21 22 23 24 25 10 9 8 7 6 5 4 3 2 1
001–325209–August/2021

DK books are available at special discounts when purchased in bulk for sales promotions, premiums, fund-raising, or educational use. For details, contact: DK Publishing Special Markets, 1450 Broadway, Suite 801, New York, NY 10018. SpecialSales@dk.com

Printed and bound in Canada

For the curious
www.dk.com

MIX
Paper from responsible sources
FSC™ C018179

This book was made with Forest Stewardship Council ™ certified paper—one small step in DK's commitment to a sustainable future. For more information go to www.dk.com/our-green-pledge